KU-417-582

THE USBORNE
FIRST THOUSAND WORDS
IN SPANISH

Heather Amery

Illustrated by Stephen Cartwright

Revised edition by Mairi Mackinnon
Picture editing by Mike Olley
Spanish language consultant: Isabel Sánchez Gallego

There is a little yellow duck to look for on every
double page with pictures. Can you find it?

Stephen Cartwright's little yellow duck made his first-ever appearance in *The First Thousand Words* over thirty years ago. Duck has since featured in over 125 titles, in more than 70 languages, and has delighted millions of readers, both young and old, around the world.

This revised edition first published in 2014 by Usborne Publishing Ltd, 83-85 Saffron Hill, London EC1N 8RT. www.usborne.com
Based on a previous title first published in 1979. Copyright © 2014,1995,1979 Usborne Publishing Ltd.

The name Usborne and the devices ♈ ⊕ are Trade Marks of Usborne Publishing Ltd. All rights reserved.
No part of this publication may be reproduced, stored in a retrieval system or transmitted in any form or by any means,
electronic, mechanical, photocopying, recording or otherwise, without the prior permission of the publisher. UKE

About this book

The First Thousand Words in Spanish is an enormously popular book that has helped many thousands of children and adults learn new words and improve their Spanish language skills.

You'll find it easy to learn words by looking at the **small labelled pictures**. Then you can practice the words by talking about the large central pictures. You can also **listen to the words** on the Usborne website (see below).

There is an alphabetical **word list** at the back of the book, which you can use to look up words in the picture pages.

Remember, this is a book of a thousand words. It will take time to learn them all.

Masculine and feminine words
When you look at Spanish words for things such as "table" or "man", you will see that they have **el** or **la** in front of them. This is because all Spanish words for people and things are either masculine or feminine. **El** is the word for "the" in front of a masculine word and **la** is "the" in front of a feminine word. For plurals (more than one, as in "tables" or "men"), the Spanish word for "the" is **los** for masculine words and **las** for feminine words.

All the labels in this book show words for things with **el**, **la**, **los** or **las**. Always learn them with this little word.

Looking at Spanish words
In Spanish, the letters **a e i o** and **u** are sometimes written with a stress mark, a sign that goes above them. This sign changes the way you say the word. Spanish also has an extra letter, which is an **n** with a sign like a squiggle over the top. This **ñ** is said "nyuh", (like the "nio" in "onion").

How to say the Spanish words
The best way to learn how to pronounce Spanish words is to listen to a native Spanish speaker. You can hear the words in this book, read by a native speaker, on the Usborne Quicklinks website. Just go to **www.usborne.com/quicklinks** and enter the keywords **1000 spanish**. There you can also find links to other useful websites about the Spanish language, Spain and Latin America.

Please note that Usborne Publishing is not responsible for the content of external websites. Please follow the internet safety guidelines on the Usborne website.

las pinturas

las botellas

los peces de colores

el helicóptero

el rompecabezas

el chocolate

La casa

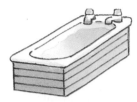
la bañera

el jabón

el grifo

el papel higiénico

el cepillo de dientes

el agua

el váter

la esponja

el lavabo

la ducha

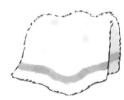
la toalla

la cama

El cuarto de baño

El cuarto de estar

la pasta de dientes

la radio

el cojín

el DVD

la moqueta

el sofá

 la silla

 el edredón

 el peine

 la sábana

la alfombra

 el armario

El dormitorio

 la televisión

 la cómoda

 el espejo

 el cepillo del pelo

 la lámpara

El vestíbulo

 los posters

 el colgador de ropa

 el teléfono

 el radiador

 la fruta

 el periódico

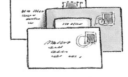 la mesa

 las cartas

 las escaleras

5

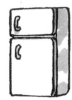

el frigorífico

los vasos

el reloj

el taburete

las cucharillas

el interruptor

el detergente

la llave

la puerta

La cocina

el fregadero

la aspiradora

las cacerolas

los tenedores

el delantal

la tabla de planchar

la basura

6

 el hervidor

los cuchillos

la fregona

 el trapo del polvo

 los azulejos

la escoba

 la lavadora

 el recogedor

 el cajón

 los platillos

 la sartén

 la cocina

las cucharas de palo

 los platos

 la plancha

 el armario

el paño de cocina

 las tazas

 los fósforos

 el cepillo

 los cuencos

7

la carretilla

la colmena

el caracol

los ladrillos

la paloma

la pala

la mariquita

el cubo de basura

las semillas

el cobertizo

El jardín

la regadera

el gusano

las flores

el aspersor

la azada

la avispa

8

la abeja

la paleta

el hueso

el seto

la horca

la cortacésped

el camino

las hojas

el árbol

el humo

la oruga

el rastrillo

el nido

los palos

la hierba

el cochecito
de niño

las verduras

la hoguera

la manguera

el invernadero

El taller

el torno de banco

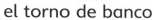

el papel de lija

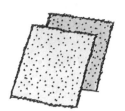

el taladro

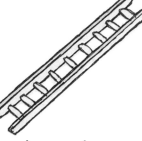

la escalera

la sierra

el serrín

el calendario

la caja de
herramientas

los tornillos

el destornillador

el tablón

las virutas

la navaja

10

las tachuelas

la araña

los tornillos
a tuerca

las tuercas

la telaraña

el barril

la mosca

el hacha

el metro

el martillo

la lima

el bote de
pintura

el cepillo de
carpintero

la madera

los clavos

la mesa de trabajo

los tarros

11

La calle

la tienda

el agujero

el café

la ambulancia

la acera

la estatua

la chimenea

el tejado

la excavadora

el hotel

el autobús

el hombre

el coche
de policía

las
tuberías

la
taladradora

el colegio

el patio
de recreo

el taxi

el paso de peatones

la fábrica

el camión

el semáforo

el cine

la camioneta

la apisonadora

el remolque

la casa

el mercado

los escalones

la moto

la bicicleta

el coche de bomberos

el policía

el coche

la mujer

la farola

los apartamentos

La juguetería

el tren

los dados

la flauta

el robot

el collar

la cámara
de fotos

las cuentas

las muñecas

la guitarra

la sortija

la casa
de muñecas

la armónica

14

el silbato

los cubos

el castillo

el submarino

la trompeta

las flechas

el arco

el paracaídas

el barco

las pinturas para la cara

la apisonadora

las máscaras

el coche de carreras

el caballo de balancín

la alcancia

las canicas

los títeres

el piano

los astronautas

la grúa

los naipes

los tambores

los soldaditos

la caja de pinturas

el cohete

15

los columpios

el hoyo de arena

el picnic

la cometa

el helado

el perro

la puerta
de la verja

el sendero

la rana

El parque

el banco

16 el tobogán

los renacuajos

el lago

los patines

el arbusto

 el bebé

 el monopatín

 la tierra

 la sillita

 el subibaja

 los niños

 el triciclo

 los pájaros

 la verja

 el balón

 el velero

 la cuerda

 el charco

 los patitos

 la cuerda de saltar

 los árboles

 el macizo de flores

los cisnes

 la correa del perro

 los patos

17

Los animales

el panda

el ala

el águila

el hipopótamo

el mono

el murciélago

el gorila

las patas

el canguro

el iceberg

el rabo

el lobo

el cocodrilo

el pingüino

las plumas

el oso

el pelícano

el avestruz

el delfín

el león

los cachorros de león

la jirafa

el ciervo

el camello

la foca

el oso polar

la tortuga

la trompa

el elefante

el rinoceronte

el bisonte

los cuernos

el castor

la cabra

la cebra

la serpiente

el tiburón

la ballena

el tigre

el leopardo

19

las vías

Los viajes

la máquina

los topes

los vagones

el maquinista

el tren de mercancías

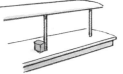
el andén

la revisora

la maleta

la máquina de billetes

La estación de ferrocarril

La estación de servicio

las señales

la mochila

los faros

el motor

la rueda

la batería

el avión

el helicóptero

la pista de aterrizaje

El aeropuerto

LAVADO DE COCHES

la torre de control

la tripulación

el piloto

el lavado de coches

el maletero

la gasolina

el camión grúa

el camión cisterna

la llave inglesa

el neumático

el capó

el aceite

el surtidor de gasolina

21

El campo

el molino
de viento

el globo
aerostático

la mariposa

la lagartija

las piedras

el zorro

el arroyo

el poste
indicador

el erizo

la esclusa

la ardilla

el bosque

el tejón

el río

la carretera

22

las tiendas de campaña

el canal

los troncos

el pueblo

la mariposa nocturna

el puente

la barcaza

la cascada

el búho

el túnel

los zorritos

el topo

el pescador

las rocas

el sapo

el tren

la caravana

la colina

23

el almiar

el perro pastor

los corderos

el estanque

los pollitos

el pajar

la pocilga

el toro

el gallinero

el tractor

La granja

el gallo

las ocas

el camión
cisterna

el granero

el lodo   la carretilla

24

 el granjero

el campo

 las gallinas

el ternero

la valla

la silla de montar

 el establo

 la vaca

 el arado

 el huerto

 la cuadra

 los cerditos

 el burro

 los pavos

 el espantapájaros

 la granja

 el heno

las ovejas

 las balas de paja

 el caballo

 los cerdos

25

La playa

el barco de vela

el mar

el remo

el faro

la pala

el cubo

la estrella
de mar

el castillo
de arena

la sombrilla

la bandera

el marinero

el molusco

el cangrejo

la gaviota

la isla

la lancha motora

el esquí
acuático

26

las olas

el sombrero
de paja

el acantilado

el barco

la canoa

la maroma

las piedrecitas

las algas

la red

el canalete
doble

el barco de
pesca

las aletas

la crema solar

el pez

el traje
de baño

el petrolero

la playa

el bote de remos

la tumbona

27

las tijeras

$$2 + 2 = 4$$
$$2 + 3 = 5$$

las sumas

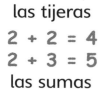

la goma de borrar

la regla

las fotos

los marcadores

la arcilla

las pinturas

el chico

el lápiz

La escuela

la pizarra

el escritorio

los libros

el bolígrafo

el pegamento

la tiza

el dibujo

28

la papelera

la profesora

la caja

el mapa

el pincel

el techo

la pared

el suelo

el cuaderno

**a b c ch d e f
g h i j k l ll m n
ñ o p q u r s t
u v w x y z**

el abecedario

la chapa

la pecera

el papel

la persiana

a b c ch d e f
g h i j k l ll m n
ñ o p q u r s t
u v w x y z

2 + 2 = 4
2 + 3 = 5

la manilla de
la puerta

la planta

el globo
terráqueo

la chica

los crayones

la lámpara

el caballete

29

El hospital

el enfermero

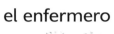
el algodón

la medicina

el ascensor

la bata

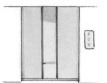
las muletas

los comprimidos

la bandeja

el reloj

el termómetro

la cortina

la manzana

la escayola

la venda

la silla
de ruedas

el rompecabezas

la médica

la jeringuilla

30

El médico

las zapatillas

el ordenador

la tirita

el plátano

las uvas

la cesta

los juguetes

la pera

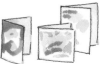
las tarjetas

el pañal

el bastón

la almohada   el camisón   el pijama   la naranja   los pañuelos de papel   la revista   la sala de espera

31

La fiesta

el globo

el chocolate

las gafas

el caramelo

la ventana

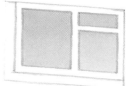

los fuegos
artificiales

la cinta

la tarta

los regalos

la pajita   la vela

la cadeneta

los juguetes

32

la mandarina

el chorizo

el osito de trapo

la salchicha

las patatas fritas

el disfraz

la cereza

el zumo

la frambuesa

la fresa

la bombilla

el bocadillo

la mantequilla

la galleta

el queso

el pan

el mantel

33

El supermercado

el pomelo

la zanahoria

la coliflor

el puerro

el champiñón

el pepino

el limón

el apio

el albaricoque

el melón

la bolsa

queso

frutas y verduras

la cebolla

la col

el melocotón

la lechuga

los guisantes

el tomate

los huevos

la ciruela

 la harina

 la balanza

 los tarros

la carne

 la piña

 el yogur

 la cesta

 las botellas

 el bolso

el monedero

 el dinero

 las latas

 el carro

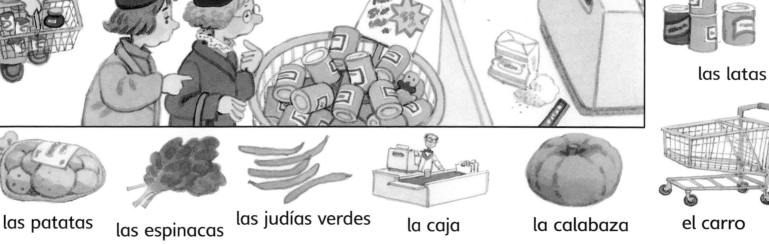

las patatas   las espinacas   las judías verdes   la caja   la calabaza

Los alimentos

la comida

el desayuno

el café

el huevo pasado por agua

el huevo frito

las tostadas

la mermelada

la nata

la leche

el cereal

el chocolate caliente

el azúcar

la miel

la sal

la pimienta

el té

la tetera

las crepes

los panecillos

la cena

el jamón

la sopa

la tortilla

la ensalada

los palillos

la hamburguesa

el pollo

el arroz

la salsa

los espaguetis

el puré de patatas

la pizza

las patatas fritas

los postres

Yo

la cabeza

el pelo

la cara

la ceja

el ojo

la nariz

la mejilla

la boca

los labios

el brazo

el codo

la barriga

los dientes

la lengua

la barbilla

las orejas

el cuello

los hombros

los dedos del pie

el pie

la pierna

la rodilla

el pecho

la espalda

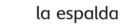
el trasero

la mano

el pulgar

los dedos

38

La ropa

los calcetines

los calzoncillos

la camiseta

los pantalones

los vaqueros

la camiseta

la falda

la camisa

la corbata

los pantalones cortos

las medias

el vestido

el jersey

la sudadera

la chaqueta de punto

la bufanda

el pañuelo

las zapatillas de deporte

los zapatos

las sandalias

las botas

los guantes

los bolsillos

el cinturón

la hebilla

la cremallera

el cordón del zapato

los botones

los ojales

el abrigo

el chaquetón

la gorra

el sombrero

La gente

el actor   la actriz

el cocinero

el bailarín

la bailarina

los cantantes

el astronauta

el carnicero

el policía

la policía

el carpintero

el bombero

la artista

el juez

el mecánico

la mecánica

el peluquero

la conductora
de camión

el conductor
de autobús

el camarero   la camarera

el cartero

la dentista

el pintor

el submarinista

la
panadera

La familia

el hijo
el hermano

la hija
la hermana

la madre
la esposa

el padre
el esposo

la tía

el tío

la
mascota

el primo

el abuelo

la abuela

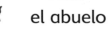

Haciendo cosas

reírse

sonreír

llorar

pensar

escuchar

coger

lanzar

romper

pintar

escribir

partir

cortar

comer

hablar

cavar

llevar

beber

hacer

saltar

bailar

lavarse

tejer

gatear

jugar

mirar

trepar

pelear

dormir

tomar

saltar a
la cuerda

coser

esperar

cocinar

esconderse

leer

comprar

cantar

empujar

barrer

recoger

soplar

tirar

caerse

caminar

correr

estar sentados

43

Palabras opuestas

bueno

malo

lejos

cerca

arriba

abajo

frío

caliente

mojado

seco

sucio

limpio

encima

debajo

gordo

delgado

abierto

cerrado

pequeño

grande

pocos

muchos

primero

último

a la izquierda

44

fuera

dentro

fácil

difícil

vacío

lleno

blando

duro

la parte delantera

alto

lento

rápido

la parte trasera

bajo

largo

corto

muerto

vivo

oscuro

claro

viejo

arriba

a la derecha

nuevo

abajo

45

Los días

lunes

martes

miércoles

jueves

viernes

sábado

domingo

el calendario

la mañana

el sol

la tarde

la noche

el espacio

el planeta

la nave espacial

la luna

la estrella

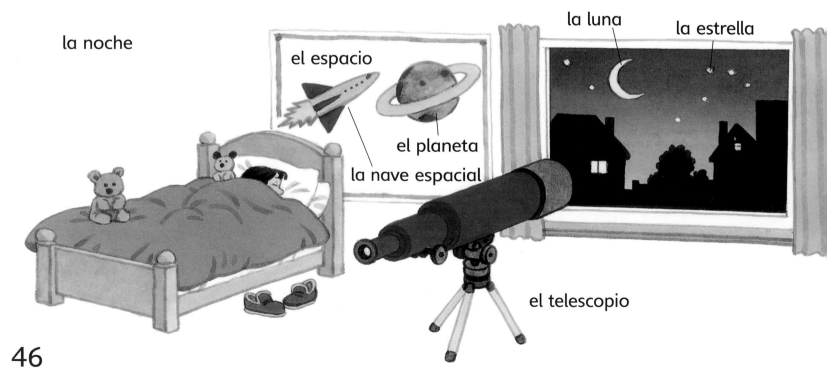

el telescopio

Días especiales

el cumpleaños

el regalo

la vela

la tarta de cumpleaños

la tarjeta de cumpleaños

las vacaciones

el día de la boda

los invitados

la dama de honor

la novia

el novio

la cámara de fotos

el fotógrafo

el día de Navidad

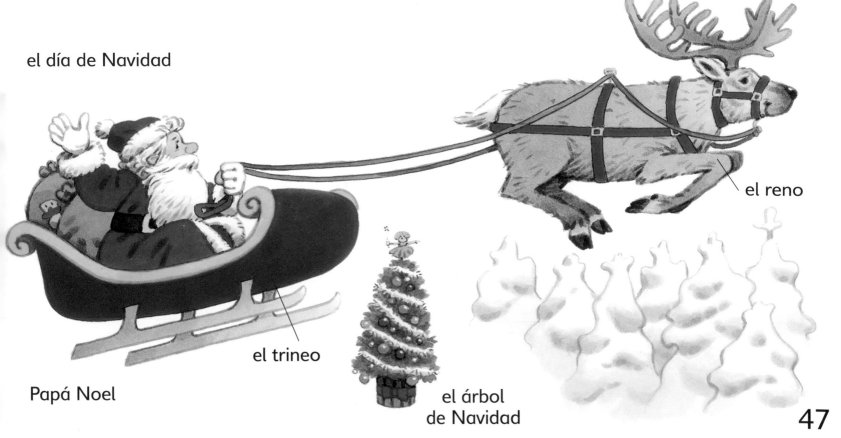

el reno

el trineo

Papá Noel

el árbol de Navidad

El tiempo

el sol

las nubes

el cielo

el paraguas

la lluvia

el relámpago

la niebla

la nieve

el rocío

el viento

la neblina

la helada

el arco iris

Las estaciones

la primavera

el verano

el otoño

el invierno

Las mascotas

la veterinaria

el hámster

la perrera

el conejillo
de Indias

el cachorro

el perro

el periquito

la comida

el loro

el pico

el conejo

el canario

la jaula

el gato

la cesta

el gatito

el ratón

la leche

los peces
de colores

49

Los deportes

el baloncesto

el remo

la vela

la vela

el windsurfing

el snowboarding

la raqueta

el tenis

el futbol americano

la gimnasia

el cricket

el karate

el bate

la pelota

el baile

el béisbol

la caña de pescar

la pesca

el anzuelo

el rugby

el salto de trampolín

la piscina

la carrera

la natación

el tiro con arco

la diana

el ala delta

correr

el ciclismo

el casco

la escalada

el judo

el caballo

el poney

la taquilla

el futbol

la equitación

el vestuario

el bádminton

el ping-pong

los patines de hielo

el patinaje sobre hielo

el palo de esquí

la telesilla

esquiar

el esquí

el sumo

51

Los colores

naranja

verde

negro

gris

rojo

marrón

rosa

violeta

amarillo

blanco

azul

Las formas

el rectángulo

el círculo

el rombo

el cono

la estrella

el cubo

el óvalo

el triángulo

el cuadrado

la media luna

Los números

1	uno
2	dos
3	tres
4	cuatro
5	cinco
6	seis
7	siete
8	ocho
9	nueve
10	diez
11	once
12	doce
13	trece
14	catorce
15	quince
16	dieciséis
17	diecisiete
18	dieciocho
19	diecinueve
20	veinte

La feria

la noria

el tiovivo

el algodón
de azúcar

el tren fantasma

las palomitas
de maíz

la colchoneta

el tobogán

los autos de choque

los aros

la montaña rusa

El circo

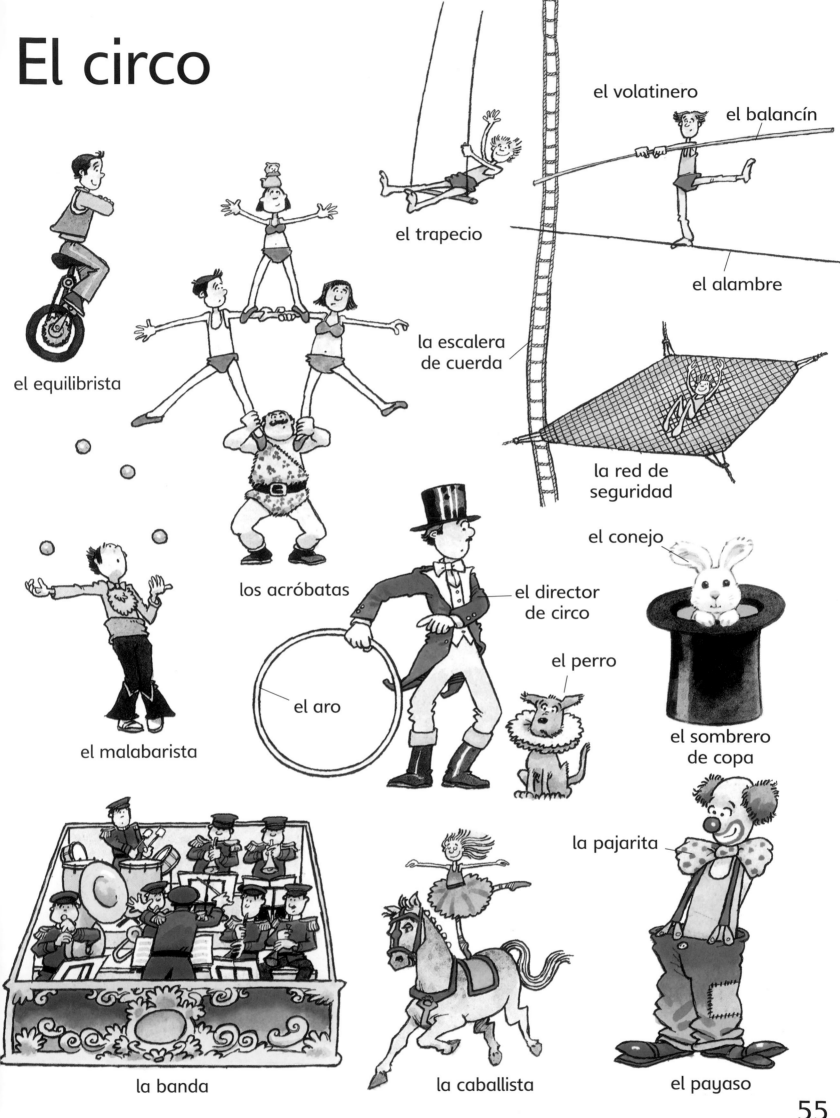

el equilibrista

el trapecio

el volatinero

el balancín

el alambre

la escalera de cuerda

la red de seguridad

el conejo

los acróbatas

el director de circo

el perro

el sombrero de copa

el malabarista

el aro

la pajarita

la banda

la caballista

el payaso

Word list

In this list, you can find all the Spanish words in this book, in alphabetical order. Next to each one, you can see its pronunciation (how to say it) in italic letters *like this*, and then its English translation.

Remember that Spanish nouns (words for things) are either masculine or feminine (see page 3). In the list, each one has **el**, **la**, **los** or **las** in front of it. These all mean "the". **El** and **los** are used in front of masculine nouns and **la** and **las** are used in front of feminine ones. **Los** and **las** are used in front of a plural noun (a noun is plural if you are talking about more than one, for example "cats").

About Spanish pronunciation
Read the pronunciation as if it were an English word, but try to remember the following rules about how Spanish words are said:

- most Spanish words have a part that you stress, or say louder (like the "day" part of the English word "today"). In the pronunciation guide, this part of the word is shown in bold letters, **like this**;
- the Spanish **r** is made by a flap of the tip of your tongue on the top of your mouth; at the beginning of the word, it is rolled like **rr** (see below);
- the Spanish **rr** is a rolled "rrrrr" sound; it is shown as "rr" in the pronunciations;
- when you see "g" in a pronunciation, say it like the "g" in "garden";
- a few Spanish letters are said differently depending on where you are in the world. When you see "th" in the pronunciation guide, in most of Spain it is said like the "th" in "thin", but in southern Spain and in Latin America, it sounds more like the "s" is "say".

A

abajo	*abaho*	bottom (not top)
el abecedario	*el abethedaree-o*	alphabet
la abeja	*la abeha*	bee
abierto	*abyairto*	open
el abrigo	*el abreego*	coat
la abuela	*la abwayla*	grandmother
el abuelo	*el abwaylo*	grandfather
el acantilado	*el akanteelado*	cliff
el aceite	*el athaytay*	oil
la acera	*la athaira*	pavement
los acróbatas	*loss akrobatass*	acrobats
el actor	*el aktor*	actor
la actriz	*la aktreeth*	actress
el aeropuerto	*el a-airopwairto*	airport
el agua	*el agwa*	water
el águila	*el ageela*	eagle
el agujero	*el agoohairo*	hole
el ala	*el ala*	wing
el ala delta	*el ala delta*	hang-gliding
el alambre	*el alambray*	tightrope
el albaricoque	*el albareekokay*	apricot
la alcancia	*la alkantheea*	money box
las aletas	*lass aletass*	flippers
la alfombra	*la alfombra*	carpet
las algas	*lass algass*	seaweed
el algodón	*el algodon*	cotton wool
el algodón de azúcar	*el algodon day athookar*	candy floss
los alimentos	*loss aleementoss*	food
el almiar	*el almee-ar*	haystack
la almohada	*la almo-ada*	pillow
alto	*alto*	high, tall
amarillo	*amareelyo*	yellow
la ambulancia	*la amboo-lanthee-a*	ambulance
andar	*andar*	to walk
andar a gatas	*andar a gatass*	to crawl
el andén	*el anden*	platform
los animales	*loss aneemalayss*	animals
el anzuelo	*el anthwaylo*	bait
el apio	*el apee-o*	celery
la apisonadora	*la apeessonadora*	roller
los apartamentos	*loss apartamentoss*	flats
el arado	*el arado*	plough
la araña	*la aranya*	spider
el árbol	*el arbol*	tree
el árbol de Navidad	*el arbol day nabeedad*	Christmas tree
los árboles	*loss arbolayss*	trees
el arbusto	*el arboossto*	bush
la arcilla	*la artheelya*	clay
el arco	*el arko*	bow
el arco iris	*el arko eereess*	rainbow
la ardilla	*la ardeelya*	squirrel
el armario	*el armaree-o*	cupboard, wardrobe
la armónica	*la armoneeka*	mouth organ
el aro	*el aro*	hoop
los aros	*loss aross*	hoop-la
arriba	*arreeba*	top, upstairs
el arroyo	*el arroyo*	stream
el arroz	*el arroth*	rice
la artista	*la arteessta*	artist (woman)
el ascensor	*el assthensor*	lift
el aspersor	*el asspersor*	sprinkler
la aspiradora	*la asspeerador*	vacuum cleaner
el astronauta	*el asstrona-oota*	astronaut
los astronautas	*loss asstrona-ootass*	spacemen
el autobús	*el a-ootobooss*	bus
los autos de choque	*loss a-ootoss day chokay*	dodgems
el avestruz	*el abesstrooth*	ostrich
el avión	*el abee-on*	plane
la avispa	*la abeesspa*	wasp
la azada	*la athada*	hoe
el azúcar	*el athookar*	sugar
azul	*athool*	blue
los azulejos	*loss athoolehoss*	tiles

B

el bádminton	*el badmeenton*	badminton
bailar	*buylar*	to dance
el bailarín	*el buylareen*	dancer (man)
la bailarina	*la buylareena*	dancer (woman)

el baile	el **buy**lay	dance
bajo	**ba**ho	low
el balancín	el balan**theen**	balancing pole
la balanza	la bala**ntha**	scales
las balas de paja	lass **ba**lass day **pa**ha	straw bales
la ballena	la bal**yena**	whale
el balón	el ba**lon**	ball
el baloncesto	el balon**thess**to	basketball
el banco	el **ban**ko	bench
la banda	la **ban**da	band
la bandeja	la ban**de**ha	tray
la bandera	la ban**dair**a	flag
la bañera	la ban**yair**a	bath
la barbilla	la bar**beel**ya	chin
la barcaza	la bar**katha**	barge
el barco	el **bar**ko	boat, ship
el barco de pesca	el **bar**ko day **pess**ka	fishing boat
el barco de vela	el **bar**ko day **bay**la	sailing boat
la barriga	la bar**ree**ga	tummy
barrer	ba**rrair**	o sweep
el barril	el ba**rreel**	barrel
el bastón	el bass**ton**	walking stick
la basura	la ba**ssoora**	rubbish
la bata	la **ba**ta	dressing gown
el bate	el **ba**tay	bat
la batería	la bate**ree**-a	battery
el bebé	el be**bay**	baby
beber	be**bair**	to drink
el béisbol	el **bayss**bol	baseball
la bicicleta	la beethee**klay**ta	bicycle
el bisonte	el bee**sson**tay	bison
blanco	**blan**ko	white
blando	**blan**do	soft
la boca	la **bo**ka	mouth
el bocadillo	el boka**deel**yo	sandwich
el bolígrafo	el bo**lee**grafo	pen
la bolsa	la **bol**ssa	bag
los bolsillos	loss bol**sseel**yoss	pockets
el bolso	el **bol**sso	handbag
el bombero	el bom**bair**o	fireman
la bombilla	la bom**beel**ya	light bulb
el bosque	el **boss**kay	forest
las botas	lass **bo**tass	boots
el bote de pintura	el **bo**tay day peen**too**ra	paint pot
el bote de remos	el **bo**tay day **ray**moss	rowing boat
las botellas	lass bo**tel**yass	bottles
los botones	loss bo**to**nayss	buttons
el brazo	el **bra**tho	arm
bueno	**bway**no	good
la bufanda	la boo**fan**da	scarf
el búho	el **boo**-o	owl
el burro	el **boo**rro	donkey

C

el caballete	el kabal**yay**tay	easel
la caballista	la kabal**yees**ta	bareback rider (woman)
el caballo	el ka**bal**yo	horse
el caballo de balancín	el ka**bal**yo day balan**theen**	rocking horse
la cabeza	la ka**betha**	head
la cabra	la **ka**bra	goat
las cacerolas	lass kathai**rol**ass	saucepans

el cachorro	el ka**chorro**	puppy
los cachorros de león	loss ka**chorros** day lay**on**	lion cubs
la cadeneta	la kade**nay**ta	paper chain
caerse	ka-**air**ssay	to fall
el café	el ka**fay**	café, coffee
la caja	la **ka**ha	box, checkout
la caja de herramientas	la **ka**ha day erram**yen**tass	tool box
la caja de pinturas	la **ka**ha day peen**too**rass	paint box
el cajón	el ka**hon**	drawer
la calabaza	la kala**batha**	pumpkin
los calcetines	loss kalthe**tee**nayss	socks
el calendario	el kalen**daree**-o	calendar
caliente	kalee-**en**tay	hot
la calle	la **kal**yay	street
los calzoncillos	loss kalthon-**theel**yoss	pants
la cama	la **ka**ma	bed
la cámara de fotos	la **ka**mara day **fo**toss	camera
la camarera	la kama**rrair**a	waitress
el camarero	el kama**rrair**o	waiter
el camello	el ka**mel**yo	camel
el camino	el ka**mee**no	path
el camión	el kamee-**on**	lorry
el camión cisterna	el kamee-**on** thees**tair**na	tanker (lorry)
el camión grúa	el kamee-**on groo**a	breakdown lorry
la camioneta	la kameeo**nay**ta	van
la camisa	la ka**meessa**	shirt
la camiseta	la kamee**ssay**ta	T-shirt, vest
el camisón	el kamee**sson**	nightdress
el campo	el **kam**po	countryside, field
la caña de pescar	la **kan**ya day pess**kar**	fishing rod
el canal	el ka**nal**	canal
el canalete doble	el kana**lay**tay **dob**lay	paddle
el canario	el ka**naree**-o	canary
el cangrejo	el kan**greho**	crab
el canguro	el kan**goo**ro	kangaroo
las canicas	lass ka**nee**kass	marbles
la canoa	la ka**no**-a	canoe
cantar	kan**tar**	to sing
los cantantes	loss kan**tan**tayss	singers
el capó	el ka**po**	(car) bonnet
la cara	la **ka**ra	face
el caracol	el kara**kol**	snail
el caramelo	el kara**may**lo	sweet
la caravana	la kara**vana**	caravan
la carne	la **kar**nay	meat
el carnicero	el karnee**thair**o	butcher
el carpintero	el karpeen**tair**o	carpenter
la carrera	la ka**rrair**a	race
la carretera	la karre**tair**a	road
la carretilla	la karre**teel**ya	wheelbarrow, cart
el carro	el **ka**rro	trolley
las cartas	lass **kar**tass	letters
el cartero	el kar**tair**o	postman
la casa	la **kas**sa	house
la casa de muñecas	la **kas**sa day moon**yek**ass	doll's house
la casa del perro	la **kas**sa del **per**ro	kennel
la cascada	la kass**kada**	waterfall
el casco	el **kass**ko	helmet
el castillo	el kas**teel**yo	castle

Spanish	Pronunciation	English
el castillo de arena	el kas**teel**yo day a**ray**na	sandcastle
el castor	el kas**tor**	beaver
catorce	ka**tor**thay	fourteen
cavar	ka**bar**	to dig
la cebolla	la the**bol**ya	onion
la cebra	la **theb**ra	zebra
la ceja	la **the**ha	eyebrow
la cena	la **thay**na	supper, dinner (evening meal)
el cepillo	el the**peel**yo	brush
el cepillo de carpintero	el the**peel**yo day karpeen**tair**o	(shaving) plane
el cepillo de dientes	el the**peel**yo day **dyen**tayss	toothbrush
el cepillo del pelo	el the**peel**yo del **pay**lo	hairbrush
cerca	**thair**ka	near
los cerditos	loss thair**dee**toss	piglets
los cerdos	loss **thair**doss	pigs
los cereales	loss there**ay**alayss	cereals
la cereza	la the**ray**tha	cherry
cerrado	ther**rad**o	closed
la cesta	la **thess**ta	basket
el champiñon	el champee**nyon**	mushroom
la chapa	la **chap**a	badge
la chaqueta de punto	la cha**ket**a day **poon**to	cardigan
el chaquetón	el chake**ton**	jacket
el charco	el **char**ko	puddle
la chica	la **chee**ka	girl
el chico	el **chee**ko	boy
la chimenea	la cheeme**nay**a	chimney
el chocolate	el choko**lat**ay	chocolate
el chocolate caliente	el choko**lat**ay kal**yen**tay	hot chocolate
el chorizo	el cho**ree**tho	salami
el ciclismo	el thee**kleez**mo	cycling
el cielo	el **thye**lo	sky
el ciervo	el **thyair**bo	deer
cinco	**theen**ko	five
el cine	el **thee**nay	cinema
la cinta	la **theen**ta	ribbon
el cinturón	el theentoo**ron**	belt
el circo	el **theer**ko	circus
el círculo	el **theer**koolo	circle
la ciruela	la theer**way**la	plum
los cisnes	loss **theess**nayss	swans
claro	**kla**ro	light (not dark)
los clavos	loss **kla**boss	nails
el cobertizo	el kobair**tee**tho	shed
el coche	el **ko**chay	car
el cochecito de niño	el koche**thee**to day **neen**yo	pram
el coche de bomberos	el **ko**chay day bom**bair**oss	fire engine
el coche de carreras	el **ko**chay day kar**rair**ass	racing car
el coche de policía	el **ko**chay day polee**thee**-a	police car
la cocina	la ko**thee**na	kitchen, cooker
cocinar	kothee**nar**	to cook
el cocinero	el kothee**nair**o	cook (man)
el cocodrilo	el koko**dree**lo	crocodile
el codo	el **ko**do	elbow
coger	ko**hair**	catch
el cohete	el ko-**ay**tay	rocket
el cojín	el ko**heen**	cushion
la col	la **kol**	cabbage
la colchoneta	la kolcho**nay**ta	mat
el colegio	el ko**lek**hyo	school
el colgador de ropa	el kolga**dor** day **ro**pa	clothes peg
la coliflor	la kolee**flor**	cauliflower
la colina	la ko**lee**na	hill
el collar	el kol**yar**	necklace
la colmena	la kol**may**na	beehive
los colores	loss ko**lor**ayss	colours
los columpios	loss ko**loom**pee-oss	swings
comer	ko**mair**	to eat
la cometa	la ko**may**ta	kite
la comida	la ko**mee**da	food, lunch, dinner (midday meal)
la cómoda	la **ko**moda	chest of drawers
comprar	kom**prar**	to buy
los comprimidos	loss compree**mee**doss	pills
la conductora de camión	la kondook**tor**a day kamee-**on**	lorry driver (woman)
el conductor de autobús	el kondook**tor** day a-ooto**booss**	bus driver
el conejillo de Indias	el kone**heel**yo day **een**deeass	guinea pig
el conejo	el kone**ho**	rabbit
el cono	el **ko**no	cone
la corbata	la kor**bat**a	tie
los corderos	loss kor**dair**os	lambs
el cordón del zapato	el kor**don** del tha**pat**o	shoelace
la correa del perro	la kor**ray**a del **pair**ro	dog lead
correr	kor**rair**	to run, jogging
la cortacésped	la korta**thess**ped	lawn mower
cortar	kor**tar**	to cut
la cortina	la kor**tee**na	curtain
corto	**kor**to	short
coser	kos**sair**	to sew
los crayones	loss kray**on**ayss	crayons
la cremallera	la kraymal**yair**a	zip
la crema solar	la **kray**ma so**lar**	suncream
los crêpes	loss **kray**payss	pancakes
el cricket	el **kree**ket	cricket (sport)
el cuaderno	el kwa**dair**no	notebook
la cuadra	la **kwa**dra	stable
el cuadrado	el kwa**drad**o	square
cuatro	**kwa**tro	four
el cuarto de baño	el **kwar**to day **ban**yo	bathroom
el cuarto de estar	el **kwar**to day ess**tar**	living room
el cubo	el **koo**bo	bucket, cube
el cubo de basura	el **koo**bo day bas**soo**ra	rubbish bin
los cubos	loss **koo**boss	(toy) bricks
las cucharas de palo	lass koo**char**ass day **pa**lo	wooden spoons
las cucharillas	lass koocha**reel**yass	teaspoons
los cuchillos	loss koo**cheel**yoss	knives
el cuello	el **kway**lyo	neck
los cuencos	loss **kwen**koss	bowls
las cuentas	lass **kwen**tass	beads
la cuerda	la **kwair**da	rope
la cuerda de saltar	la **kwair**da day sal**tar**	skipping rope
los cuernos	loss **kwair**noss	horns
el cumpleaños	el koomplay-**an**yoss	birthday

D

los dados	*loss **da**doss*	dice
la dama de honor	*la **da**ma day o**nor***	bridesmaid
debajo	*de**ba**ho*	under
los dedos	*loss **day**doss*	fingers
los dedos del pie	*loss **day**doss del **pyay***	toes
el delantal	*el delan**tal***	apron
el delfín	*el del**feen***	dolphin
delgado	*del**ga**do*	thin
la dentista	*la den**teess**ta*	dentist (woman)
dentro	***den**tro*	in
los deportes	*loss de**por**tayss*	sports
a la derecha	*a la de**re**cha*	(on/to the) right
el desayuno	*el dessa-**yoo**no*	breakfast
el destornillador	*el desstorneelya**dor***	screwdriver
el detergente	*el detair**hen**tay*	washing powder
el día de la boda	*el **dee**a day la **bo**da*	wedding day
el día de Navidad	*el **dee**a day nabee**dad***	Christmas Day
la diana	*la dee-**a**na*	target
los días	*loss **dee**ass*	days
días especiales	***dee**ass esspethee-**a**layss*	special days
el dibujo	*el dee**boo**ho*	drawing
diecinueve	*dee-ethee-**nway**bay*	nineteen
dieciocho	*dee-ethee-**o**cho*	eighteen
dieciséis	*dee-ethee-**ssayss***	sixteen
diecisiete	*dee-ethee-**ssyay**tay*	seventeen
los dientes	*loss dee-**en**tayss*	teeth
diez	*dee-**eth***	ten
difícil	*dee**fee**theel*	difficult
el dinero	*el dee**nai**ro*	money
el director de circo	*el deerek**tor** day **theer**ko*	ring master
el disfraz	*el dees**frath***	costume
doce	***do**thay*	twelve
domingo	*do**meen**go*	Sunday
dormir	*dor**meer***	to sleep
el dormitorio	*el dormee**to**ree-o*	bedroom
dos	***doss***	two
la ducha	*la **doo**cha*	shower
duro	***doo**ro*	hard
el DVD	*el daybay**day***	DVD

E

el edredón	*el edre**don***	duvet
el elefante	*el ele**fan**tay*	elephant
empujar	*empoo**har***	to push
encima	*en**thee**ma*	over
el enfermero	*el enfair**mai**ro*	nurse (man)
la ensalada	*la enssa**la**da*	salad
el equilibrista	*el ekeelee**brees**ta*	trick cyclist
la equitación	*la ekeetathee-**on***	riding
el erizo	*el e**ree**tho*	hedgehog
la escalada	*la esska**la**da*	climbing
la escalera	*la esska**lai**ra*	ladder
la escalera de cuerda	*la esska**lai**ra day **kwair**da*	rope ladder
las escaleras	*lass esska**lai**rass*	stairs
los escalones	*loss esska**lo**nayss*	steps
la escayola	*la esska**yo**la*	cast
la esclusa	*la ess**kloo**ssa*	(canal) lock
la escoba	*la ess**ko**ba*	broom
esconderse	*esskon**dair**ssay*	to hide
escribir	*esskree**beer***	to write
el escritorio	*el esskree**to**reeo*	desk
escuchar	*esskoo**char***	to listen
la escuela	*la ess**kway**la*	school
el espacio	*el ess**pa**thee-o*	space
los espaguetis	*loss esspa**ge**teess*	spaghetti
la espalda	*la ess**pal**da*	back (of body)
el espantapájaros	*el esspanta-**pa**haross*	scarecrow
el espejo	*el ess**pe**ho*	mirror
esperar	*esspe**rar***	to wait
las espinacas	*lass esspee**na**kass*	spinach
la esponja	*la ess**pon**ha*	sponge
la esposa	*la ess**po**ssa*	wife
el esposo	*el ess**po**sso*	husband
el esquí	*el ess**kee***	ski
el esquí acuático	*el ess**kee** **kwa**teeko*	water-skiing
esquiar	*esskee**ar***	skiing
el establo	*el ess**ta**blo*	cowshed
la estación de ferrocarril	*la estasthee-**on** day ferrokar**reel***	railway station
la estación de servicio	*la estasthee-**on** day ser**vee**heeo*	garage (petrol station)
las estaciones	*lass esstathee-**o**nayss*	seasons
el estanque	*el ess**tan**kay*	pond
estar sentados	*ess**tar** sen**ta**doss*	to sit
la estátua	*la ess**ta**tooa*	statue
la estrella	*la ess**tray**lya*	star
la estrella de mar	*la ess**tray**lya day **mar***	starfish
la excavadora	*la ekskaba**do**ra*	digger

F

la fábrica	*la **fa**breeka*	factory
fácil	***fa**theel*	easy
la falda	*la **fal**da*	skirt
la familia	*la fa**mee**leea*	family
el faro	*el **fa**ro*	lighthouse
la farola	*la fa**ro**la*	lamp post
los faros	*los **fa**ross*	headlights
la feria	*la **fai**ree-a*	fair, fairground
la fiesta	*la **fyess**ta*	party
la flauta	*la **fla**-oota*	recorder
las flechas	*lass **fle**chass*	arrows
las flores	*lass **flo**rayss*	flowers
la foca	*la **fo**ka*	seal
las formas	*lass **for**mass*	shapes
los fósforos	*loss **foss**foross*	matches
el fotógrafo	*el fo**to**grafo*	photographer
las fotos	*lass **fo**toss*	photographs
la frambuesa	*la fram**bway**ssa*	raspberry
el fregadero	*el frega**dai**ro*	sink
la fregona	*la fre**go**na*	mop
la fresa	*la **fray**ssa*	strawberry
el frigorífico	*el freego**ree**feeko*	fridge
frío	***free**-o*	cold
la fruta	*la **froo**ta*	fruit
los fuegos artificiales	*loss **fway**goss arteefeethee-**a**layss*	fireworks
fuera	***fwai**ra*	out
el fútbol	*el **foot**bol*	football
el fútbol americano	*el **foot**bol ameree**ka**no*	American football

G

las gafas	*lass **ga**fass*	glasses (to wear)
la galleta	*la gal**ye**ta*	biscuit
las gallinas	*lass gal**yee**nass*	hens
el gallinero	*el galyee**nai**ro*	henhouse
el gallo	*el **gal**yo*	cock
la gasolina	*la gaso**lee**na*	petrol

el gatito	*el ga**tee**to*	kitten
el gato	*el **ga**to*	cat
la gaviota	*la gabee-**ota***	seagull
la gente	*la **hen**tay*	people
la gimnasia	*la heem**nass**ee-a*	gym (gymnastics)
el globo	*el **glo**bo*	balloon
el globo aerostático	*el **glo**bo a-erosta**teeko***	hot-air balloon
el globo terráqueo	*el **glo**bo terra**kay**-o*	globe
la goma de borrar	*la **go**ma day bor**rar***	rubber
gordo	***gor**do*	fat
el gorila	*el go**ree**la*	gorilla
la gorra	*la **gor**ra*	cap
grande	***gran**day*	big
el granero	*el gra**nairo***	barn
la granja	*la **gran**ha*	farm, farmhouse
el granjero	*el gran**hairo***	farmer
el grifo	*el **gree**fo*	tap
gris	***greess***	grey
la grúa	*la **groo**-a*	crane
los guantes	*loss **gwan**tayss*	gloves
los guijarros	*loss gee**harross***	pebbles
los guisantes	*loss gee**ssan**tayss*	peas
la guitarra	*la gee**tarra***	guitar
el gusano	*el **goossa**no*	worm

H

hablar	*a**blar***	to talk
hacer	*a**thair***	to make, to do
el hacha	*el **a**cha*	axe
haciendo cosas	*a**thyen**do **ko**ssass*	doing things
la hamburguesa	*la amboor**gayssa***	hamburger
el hámster	*el **am**stair*	hamster
la harina	*la a**ree**na*	flour
la hebilla	*la e**beel**ya*	buckle
la helada	*la e**la**da*	frost
el helado	*el e**la**do*	ice cream
el helicóptero	*el elee**kop**tairo*	helicopter
el heno	*el **ay**no*	hay
la hermana	*la air**ma**na*	sister
el hermano	*el air**ma**no*	brother
el hervidor	*el ervee**dor***	kettle
la hierba	*la **yair**ba*	grass
la hija	*la **ee**ha*	daughter
el hijo	*el **ee**ho*	son
el hipopótamo	*el eepo**po**tamo*	hippopotamus
la hoguera	*la o**gai**ra*	bonfire
las hojas	*lass **o**hass*	leaves
el hombre	*el **om**bray*	man
los hombros	*loss **om**bross*	shoulders
la horca	*la **or**ka*	fork
el hospital	*el osspee**tal***	hospital
el hotel	*el o**tel***	hotel
el hoyo de arena	*el **o**yo day a**ray**na*	sandpit
el huerto	*el **wair**to*	orchard
el hueso	*el **way**sso*	bone
el huevo frito	*el **way**bo **free**to*	fried egg
el huevo pasado por agua	*el **way**bo pa**ssa**do por **a**gwa*	boiled egg
los huevos	*loss **way**boss*	eggs
el humo	*el **oo**mo*	smoke

I

el iceberg	*el **eyss**berg*	iceberg
el interruptor	*el eentairoop**tor***	switch
el invernadero	*el eenbairna**dai**ro*	greenhouse
el invierno	*el een**byair**no*	winter

los invitados	*loss eenvee**ta**doss*	guests
la isla	*la **eess**la*	island
a la izquierda	*a la eeth**kyair**da*	(on/to the) left

J

el jabón	*el ha**bon***	soap
el jamón	*el ha**mon***	ham
el jardín	*el har**deen***	garden
la jaula	*la **how**la*	cage
la jeringuilla	*la hereen**geel**ya*	syringe
el jersey	*el hair**ssay***	jumper
la jirafa	*la hee**ra**fa*	giraffe
el judo	*el **joo**do*	judo
las judías verdes	*lass hoo**dee**ass **bair**dayss*	green beans
jueves	***hway**bayss*	Thursday
el juez	*el **hwayth***	judge
jugar	*hoo**gar***	to play
los juguetes	*loss hoo**gay**tayss*	toys
la juguetería	*la hoogetai**ree**-a*	toy shop

K

el kárate	*el **ka**ratay*	karate

L

los labios	*loss **la**byoss*	lips
los ladrillos	*loss la**dreel**yoss*	bricks
la lagartija	*la lagar**tee**ha*	lizard
el lago	*el **la**go*	lake
la lámpara	*la **lam**para*	lamp
la lancha motora	*la **lan**cha mo**to**ra*	speedboat
lanzar	*lan**thar***	to throw
el lápiz	*el **la**peeth*	pencil
largo	***lar**go*	long
las latas	*lass **la**tass*	tins
el lavabo	*el la**ba**bo*	washbasin
el lavado de coches	*el la**ba**do day **ko**chayss*	car wash
la lavadora	*la laba**do**ra*	washing machine
lavarse	*la**bar**ssay*	to wash (yourself)
la leche	*la **lay**chay*	milk
la lechuga	*la lay**choo**ga*	lettuce
leer	*lay**air***	to read
lejos	***lay**hoss*	far
la lengua	*la **len**gwa*	tongue
lento	***len**to*	slow
el león	*el lay**on***	lion
el leopardo	*el layo**par**do*	leopard
los libros	*loss **lee**bross*	books
la lima	*la **lee**ma*	file
el limón	*el lee**mon***	lemon
limpio	***leem**pee-o*	clean
la llave	*la **lya**bay*	key
la llave inglesa	*la **lya**bay een**glayssa***	spanner
lleno	***lye**no*	full
llevar	*lye**bar***	to carry
llorar	*lyo**rar***	to cry
la lluvia	*la **lyoo**bee-a*	rain
el lobo	*el **lo**bo*	wolf
el lodo	*el **lo**do*	mud
el loro	*el **lo**ro*	parrot
la luna	*la **loo**na*	moon
lunes	***loo**nayss*	Monday

M

el macizo de flores	*el ma**thee**tho day **flo**rayss*	flower bed

Spanish	Pronunciation	English
la madera	*la ma**dair**a*	wood
la madre	*la **ma**dray*	mother
el malabarista	*el malaba**reess**ta*	juggler
la maleta	*la ma**lay**ta*	suitcase
el maletero	*el malay**tair**o*	boot (of car)
malo	***ma**lo*	bad
la mañana	*la man**ya**na*	morning
la mandarina	*la manda**ree**na*	clementine
la manguera	*la man**gair**a*	hose
la manilla de la puerta	*la ma**neel**ya day la **pwair**ta*	door handle
la mano	*la **ma**no*	hand
el mantel	*el man**tel***	tablecloth
la mantequilla	*la mante**keel**ya*	butter
la manzana	*la man**tha**na*	apple
el mapa	*el **ma**pa*	map
la máquina	*la **ma**keena*	engine
la máquina de billetes	*la **ma**keena day beel**yay**tayss*	ticket machine
el maquinista	*el makee**neess**ta*	train driver
el mar	*el **mar***	sea
los marcadores	*loss marca**dor**ayss*	felt-tips
el marinero	*el maree**nair**o*	sailor
la mariposa	*la maree**poss**a*	butterfly
la mariposa nocturna	*la maree**poss**a nok**toor**na*	moth
la mariquita	*la maree**kee**ta*	ladybird
la maroma	*la ma**ro**ma*	rope
marrón	*ma**rron***	brown
martes	***mar**tayss*	Tuesday
el martillo	*el mar**teel**yo*	hammer
las máscaras	*lass **mass**karass*	masks
la mascota	*la mass**kot**a*	pet
las mascotas	*lass mass**kot**ass*	pets
la mecánica	*la meka**nee**ka*	mechanic (woman)
el mecánico	*el meka**nee**ko*	mechanic (man)
la media luna	*la **me**deea **loo**na*	crescent
las medias	*lass **me**deeass*	tights
la médica	*la **me**deeka*	doctor (woman)
la medicina	*la medee**thee**na*	medicine
el médico	*el **me**deeko*	doctor (man)
la mejilla	*la me**heel**ya*	cheek
el melocotón	*el meloko**ton***	peach
el melón	*el me**lon***	melon
el mercado	*el mair**ka**do*	market
la mermelada	*la mairmay**la**da*	jam
la mesa	*la **may**ssa*	table
la mesa de trabajo	*la **may**ssa day tra**ba**ho*	workbench
el metro	*el **may**tro*	tape measure
la miel	*la **my**el*	honey
miércoles	***my**air**kolayss*	Wednesday
mirar	*mee**rar***	to watch
la mochila	*la mo**chee**la*	backpack
mojado	*mo**ha**do*	wet
el molino de viento	*el mo**lee**no day **byen**to*	windmill
el molusco	*el mo**loos**sko*	seashell
el monedero	*el mone**dair**o*	purse
el mono	*el **mo**no*	monkey
el monopatín	*el monopa**teen***	skateboard
la montaña	*la mon**tan**ya*	mountain
la montaña rusa	*la mon**tan**ya **roo**ssa*	big dipper
la moqueta	*la mo**kay**ta*	carpet
la mosca	*la **moss**ka*	fly
la moto	*la **mo**to*	motorbike
el motor	*el mo**tor***	engine
muchos	***moo**choss*	many
muerto	***mwair**to*	dead
la mujer	*la moo**hair***	woman
las muletas	*lass moo**let**ass*	crutches
las muñecas	*lass moo**nyay**kass*	dolls
el murciélago	*el moor**thyay**lago*	bat

N

los naipes	*los **na**-eepayss*	playing cards
naranja	*na**ran**ha*	orange (colour)
la naranja	*la na**ran**ha*	orange (fruit)
la nariz	*el na**reeth***	nose
la nata	*la **nat**a*	cream
la natación	*la nata**thyon***	swimming
la navaja	*la na**ba**ha*	penknife
la nave espacial	*la **na**bay espathee-**al***	spaceship
la neblina	*la ne**blee**na*	mist
negro	***neg**ro*	black
el neumático	*el nayoo**ma**teeko*	tyre
el nido	*el **nee**do*	nest
la niebla	*la **nye**bla*	fog
la nieve	*la **nyay**bay*	snow
los niños	*loss **neen**yoss*	children
la noche	*la **no**chay*	night
la noria	*la **no**ree-a*	big wheel
la novia	*la **no**bee-a*	bride
el novio	*el **no**bee-o*	bridegroom
las nubes	*lass **noo**bayss*	clouds
nueve	***nway**bay*	nine
nuevo	***nway**bo*	new
los números	*loss **noo**maiross*	numbers

O

las ocas	*lass **o**kass*	geese
ocho	***o**cho*	eight
los ojales	*loss o**ha**layss*	button holes
el ojo	*el **o**ho*	eye
las olas	*lass **o**lass*	waves
once	***on**thay*	eleven
el ordenador	*el ordena**dor***	computer
las orejas	*lass o**ray**hass*	ears
la oruga	*la o**roo**ga*	caterpillar
oscuro	*oss**koo**ro*	dark
el osito de trapo	*el o**ssee**to day **tra**po*	teddy bear
el oso	*el **o**sso*	bear
el oso polar	*el **o**sso po**lar***	polar bear
el otoño	*el o**ton**yo*	autumn
el óvalo	*el **o**balo*	oval
las ovejas	*lass o**be**hass*	sheep

P

el padre	*el **pa**dray*	father
el pajar	*el pa**har***	hayloft
los pájaros	*loss **pa**haross*	birds
la pajarita	*la paha**ree**ta*	bow tie
la pajita	*la pa**hee**ta*	(drinking) straw
la pala	*la **pa**la*	spade
palabras opuestas	*pala**brass** op**wess**tass*	opposite words
la paleta	*la pa**let**a*	trowel
los palillos	*loss pa**leel**yoss*	chopsticks
el palo de esquí	*el **pa**lo day ess**kee***	ski pole
la paloma	*la pa**lo**ma*	pigeon
las palomitas de maíz	*lass palo**mee**tass day ma**eeth***	popcorn
los palos	*loss **pa**loss*	sticks

Spanish	Pronunciation	English
el pan	el **pan**	bread
la panadera	la pana**daira**	baker (woman)
el pañal	el pa**nyal**	nappy
el panda	el **pan**da	panda
los panecillos	loss pane**theel**yoss	(bread) rolls
los pantalones	loss panta**lo**nayss	trousers
los pantalones cortos	loss panta**lo**nayss **kor**toss	shorts
el paño de cocina	el **pan**yo day ko**thee**na	tea towel
el pañuelo	el paniu**way**lo	handkerchief
los pañuelos de papel	loss paniu**way**loss day pa**pel**	tissues
Papá Noel	papa noel	Father Christmas
el papel	el pa**pel**	paper
el papel de lija	el pa**pel** day **lee**ha	sandpaper
la papelera	la pape**laira**	wastepaper bin
el papel higiénico	el pa**pel** ee**hyen**eeko	toilet paper
el paracaídas	el paraka-**ee**dass	parachute
el paraguas	el para**g**wass	umbrella
la pared	la pa**raid**	wall
el parque	el **par**kay	park
la parte delantera	la **par**tay daylan**taira**	front
la parte trasera	la **par**tay tras**saira**	back
partir	par**teer**	to chop
el paso de peatones	el **pas**so day paya**to**nayss	pedestrian crossing
la pasta de dientes	la **pas**ta day **dyen**tayss	toothpaste
las patas	lass **pa**tass	paws
las patatas	lass pa**ta**tass	potatoes
las patatas fritas	lass pa**ta**tass **free**tass	crisps, chips
el patinaje sobre hielo	el pa**teen**ahay **sobray yay**lo	ice-skating
los patines	loss pa**teen**ayss	roller blades
los patines de hielo	loss pa**teen**ayss day **yay**lo	ice skates
el patio de recreo	el **pa**tee-o day re**krayo**	playground
los patitos	loss pa**teet**oss	ducklings
los patos	loss **pa**toss	ducks
los pavos	loss **pa**boss	turkeys
el payaso	el pa**yas**so	clown
la pecera	la pay**thaira**	aquarium
los peces de colores	loss **pay**thayss day ko**lor**ayss	goldfish
el pecho	el **pay**cho	chest
el pegamento	el pega**men**to	glue
el peine	el **pay**nay	comb
pelear	pela**yar**	to fight
el pelícano	el pelee**ka**no	pelican
el pelo	el **pay**lo	hair
la pelota	la pe**lo**ta	(small) ball
el peluquero	el peloo**kairo**	hairdresser (man)
pensar	pen**sar**	to think
el pepino	el pe**pee**no	cucumber
pequeño	pe**ken**yo	small
la pera	la **pair**a	pear
el periódico	el pairee-**o**deeko	newspaper
el periquito	el pairee**KEE**to	budgerigar
el perro	el **pair**ro	dog
el perro pastor	el **pair**ro pas**tor**	sheepdog
la persiana	la pairsee-**a**na	(window) blind
la pesca	la **pess**ka	fishing
el pescador	el pess**ka**dor	fisherman
el petrolero	el petro**lairo**	oil tanker (ship)
el pez	el **peth**	fish
el piano	el pee-**ano**	piano
el picnic	el **peek**neek	picnic
el pico	el **pee**ko	beak
el pie	el pee-**ay**	foot
las piedras	lass **pyed**rass	stones
la pierna	la **pyair**na	leg
el pijama	el pee**ha**ma	pyjamas
el piloto	el pee**lo**to	pilot
la pimienta	la pee**myen**ta	pepper
la piña	la **pee**nya	pineapple
el pincel	el peen**thel**	brush
el ping-pong	el **peeng-pong**	table tennis
el pingüino	el peen**gwee**no	penguin
pintar	peen**tar**	to paint
el pintor	el peen**tor**	painter
las pinturas	lass peen**too**rass	paints
las pinturas para la cara	lass peen**too**rass para la **ka**ra	face paints
la piscina	la peess**thee**na	swimming pool
la pista de aterrizaje	la **pees**ta day aterree**tha**hay	runway
la pizarra	la pee**tharra**	blackboard
la pizza	la **peet**za	pizza
la plancha	la **plan**cha	iron
el planeta	el pla**nay**ta	planet
la planta	la **plan**ta	plant
el plátano	el **pla**tano	banana
los platillos	loss pla**teel**yoss	saucers
los platos	loss **pla**toss	plates
la playa	la **pla**-ya	beach, seaside
las plumas	lass **ploo**mass	feathers
la pocilga	la po**theel**ga	pigsty
pocos	**po**koss	few
el policía	el polee**thee**-a	policeman
la policía	la polee**thee**-a	policewoman
los pollitos	loss pol**yee**toss	chicks
el pollo	el **pol**yo	chicken
el pomelo	el po**may**lo	grapefruit
el poney	el **ponee**	pony
el poste indicador	el **poss**tay eendeeka**dor**	signpost
los posters	loss **poss**tairss	pictures
los postres	loss **poss**trayss	pudding, dessert
la primavera	la preema**vaira**	spring
primero	pree**mairo**	first
el primo	el **pree**mo	cousin (boy)
la profesora	la profe**ssora**	teacher (woman)
el pueblo	el **pway**blo	village
el puente	el **pwen**tay	bridge
el puerro	el **pwair**ro	leek
la puerta	la **pwair**ta	door
la puerta de la verja	la **pwair**ta day la **bair**ha	gate
el pulgar	el **pool**gar	thumb
el puré de patatas	el poo**ray** day pa**ta**tass	mashed potatoes

Q

Spanish	Pronunciation	English
el queso	el **kay**sso	cheese
quince	**keen**thay	fifteen

R

Spanish	Pronunciation	English
el rabo	el **rabo**	tail
el radiador	el radeea**dor**	radiator

Spanish	Pronunciation	English
la radio	la **ra**dee-o	radio
la rana	la **ra**na	frog
rápido	**ra**peedo	fast
la raqueta	la ra**kay**ta	racket
el rastrillo	el ras**treel**yo	rake
el ratón	el ra**ton**	mouse
el recogedor	el rekohe**dor**	dustpan
el rectángulo	el rec**tan**goolo	rectangle
la red	la **rayd**	net
la red de seguridad	la **rayd** day segooree**dad**	safety net
la regadera	la rayga**daira**	watering can
el regalo	el ray**ga**lo	present
los regalos	loss ray**ga**loss	presents
la regla	la **ray**gla	ruler
reirse	ray-**eer**ssay	to laugh
el relámpago	el ray**lam**pago	lightning
el reloj	el ray**loh**	clock, watch
el remo	el **ray**mo	oar, paddle, rowing
el remolque	el ray**mol**kay	trailer
los renacuajos	loss rayna**kwa**hoss	tadpoles
el reno	el **ray**no	reindeer
la revisora	la rebee**ssor**a	ticket collector (woman)
la revista	la re**bees**ta	magazine
el rinoceronte	el reenothai**ron**tay	rhinoceros
el río	el **ree**-o	river
el robot	el ro**bot**	robot
las rocas	lass **ro**kass	rocks
el rocío	el ro**thee**-o	dew
la rodilla	la ro**deel**ya	knee
rojo	**ro**ho	red
el rombo	el **rom**bo	diamond
el rompecabezas	el rompay-ka**bay**thass	jigsaw
romper	rom**pair**	to break
la ropa	la **ro**pa	clothes
rosa	**ro**ssa	pink
la rueda	la **rway**da	wheel
el rugby	el **roog**bee	rugby

S

Spanish	Pronunciation	English
sábado	**sa**bado	Saturday
la sábana	la **sa**bana	sheet
la sal	la **sal**	salt
la sala de espera	la **sa**la day es**spair**a	waiting room
la salchicha	la sal**chee**cha	sausage
la salsa	la **sal**ssa	sauce
saltar	sal**tar**	to jump
saltar a la cuerda	sal**tar** a la **kwair**da	to skip
el salto de trampolín	el **sal**to day trampo**leen**	diving
las sandalias	lass san**da**lee-ass	sandals
el sapo	el **sa**po	toad
la sartén	la sar**ten**	frying pan
seco	**say**ko	dry
seis	**sayss**	six
el semáforo	el se**ma**foro	traffic lights
las semillas	lass se**meel**yas	seeds
las señales	lass se**nya**layss	signals
el sendero	el sen**dair**o	path
la serpiente	la sair**pyen**tay	snake
el serrín	el sair**reen**	sawdust
el seto	el **say**to	hedge
la sierra	la **syair**ra	saw
siete	**syay**tay	seven

Spanish	Pronunciation	English
el silbato	el seel**ba**to	whistle
la silla	la **seel**ya	chair
la silla de montar	la **seel**ya day mon**tar**	saddle
la silla de ruedas	la **seel**ya day **rway**dass	wheelchair
la sillita	la seel**yee**ta	push chair
el snowboarding	el es**snow**bordeeng	snowboarding
el sofá	el so**fa**	sofa
el sol	el **sol**	sun
los soldaditos	loss solda**dee**toss	toy soldiers
el sombrero	el som**brair**o	hat
el sombrero de copa	el som**brair**o day **ko**pa	top hat
el sombrero de paja	el som**brair**o day **pa**ha	straw hat
la sombrilla	la som**breel**ya	beach umbrella
sonreir	sonray-**eer**	to smile
la sopa	la **so**pa	soup
soplar	so**plar**	to blow
la sortija	la sor**tee**ha	ring
el subibaja	el soobee**ba**ha	seesaw
el submarinista	el sobmaree-**neess**ta	diver
el submarino	el soobma**ree**no	submarine
sucio	**soo**thee-o	dirty
la sudadera	la sooda**daira**	sweatshirt
el suelo	el **sway**lo	floor
las sumas	lass **soo**mass	sums
el sumo	el **soo**mo	jsumo wrestling
el supermercado	el soopairmair**ka**do	supermarket
el surtidor de gasolina	el soortee**dor** day gaso**lee**na	petrol pump

T

Spanish	Pronunciation	English
la tabla de planchar	la **ta**bla day plan**char**	ironing board
el tablón	el ta**blon**	plank
el taburete	el taboo**ray**tay	stool
las tachuelas	lass tach**way**lass	tacks
la taladradora	la taladra**dora**	road drill
el taladro	el ta**la**dro	drill
el taller	el tal**yair**	workshop
los tambores	loss tam**bor**ayss	drums
la taquilla	la ta**keel**ya	locker
la tarde	la **tar**day	evening
la tarjeta de cumpleaños	la tar**hay**ta day koomplay-**any**oss	birthday card
las tarjetas	lass tar**hay**tass	cards
los tarros	loss **tar**ross	jars
la tarta	la **tar**ta	cake
la tarta de cumpleaños	la **tar**ta day koomplay-**any**oss	birthday cake
el taxi	el **tak**ssee	taxi
las tazas	lass **ta**thass	cups
el té	el **tay**	tea
el techo	el **te**cho	ceiling
el tejado	el te**ha**do	roof
tejer	te**hair**	to knit
el tejón	el te**hon**	badger
la telaraña	la tela**ran**ya	cobweb
el teléfono	el te**lay**fono	telephone
el telescopio	el teles**ko**pee-o	telescope
la telesilla	la tele**seel**ya	chairlift
la televisión	la telebeessee-**on**	television
los tenedores	loss tene**dor**ayss	forks
el tenis	el **te**neess	tennis
el termómetro	el tair**mo**metro	thermometer

63

Spanish	Pronunciation	English
el ternero	el tair**nair**o	calf
la tetera	la te**tair**a	teapot
la tía	la **tee**-a	aunt
el tiburón	el teeboo**ron**	shark
el tiempo	el **tyem**po	weather
la tienda	la **tyen**da	shop
las tiendas de campaña	lass **tyen**dass day kam**pan**ya	tents
la tierra	la **tyair**ra	earth
el tigre	el **tee**gray	tiger
las tijeras	lass tee**hair**ass	scissors
el tío	el **tee**-o	uncle
el tiovivo	el teeo**bee**bo	roundabout
tirar	tee**rar**	to pull
la tirita	la tee**ree**ta	sticking plaster
el tiro con arco	el **tee**ro kon **ar**ko	archery
los títeres	loss **tee**terayss	puppets
la tiza	la **tee**tha	chalk
la toalla	la to-**al**ya	towel
el tobogán	el tobo**gan**	helter-skelter, slide
tomar	to**mar**	to take
el tomate	el to**ma**tay	tomato
los topes	loss **top**ess	buffers
el topo	el **to**po	mole
los tornillos	loss tor**neel**yoss	screws
los tornillos a tuerca	loss tor**neel**yoss a **twair**ka	bolts
el torno de banco	el **tor**no day **ban**ko	vice
el toro	el **to**ro	bull
la torre de control	la **tor**ray day kon**trol**	control tower
la tortilla	la tor**teel**ya	omelette
la tortuga	la tor**too**ga	tortoise
las tostadas	lass toss**ta**dass	toast
el tractor	el trak**tor**	tractor
el traje de baño	el **tra**hay day **ban**yo	swimsuit
el trapecio	el tra**pe**thee-o	trapeze
el trapo del polvo	el **tra**po del **pol**bo	duster
el trasero	el tra**ssair**o	bottom (body)
trece	**tray**thay	thirteen
el tren	el **tren**	train
el tren de mercancías	el **tren** day mairkan**thee**-ass	goods train
el tren fantasma	el **tren** fan**tass**ma	ghost train
trepar	tre**par**	to climb
tres	**trayss**	three
el triángulo	el tree-**an**goolo	triangle
el triciclo	el tree**thee**klo	tricycle
el trineo	el tree**nay**o	sleigh
la tripulación	la treepoola-**thyon**	cabin crew
la trompa	la **trom**pa	trunk
la trompeta	la trom**pay**ta	trumpet
los troncos	loss **tron**koss	logs
las tuberías	lass toobai**ree**-ass	pipes
las tuercas	lass **twair**kass	nuts (nuts and bolts)
la tumbona	la toom**bo**na	deck chair
el túnel	el **too**nel	tunnel

U

Spanish	Pronunciation	English
último	**ool**teemo	last
uno	**oo**no	one
las uvas	lass **oo**bass	grapes

V

la vaca	la **ba**ka	cow
las vacaciones	lass bakathee-**o**nayss	holiday
vacío	ba**thee**-o	empty
los vagones	loss ba**go**nayss	carriages
la valla	la **bal**ya	fence
los vaqueros	loss ba**kair**oss	jeans, cowboys
los vasos	loss **bass**oss	glasses (drinking)
el váter	el **ba**tair	twenty
veinte	**bay**intay	toilet
la vela	la **bay**la	candle, sail, sailing
el velero	el be**lair**o	sailing boat
la venda	la **ben**da	bandage
la ventana	la ben**ta**na	window
las verduras	lass bair**door**ass	vegetables
el verano	el bai**ra**no	summer
verde	**bair**day	green
la verja	la **bair**ha	railings
el vestíbulo	el bess**tee**boolo	hall
el vestido	el bess**tee**do	dress
el vestuario	el besstoo-**a**reeo	changing room
la veterinaria	la beteree-**nair**eea	vet (woman)
los viajes	loss bee-**a**hayss	travel
las vías	las **bee**ass	railway track
viejo	bee-**ay**ho	old
el viento	el **byen**to	wind
viernes	by**air**nayss	Friday
violeta	beeo**layt**a	purple
las virutas	lass bee**roo**tass	shavings
vivo	**bee**bo	alive
el volatinero	el bolatee**nair**o	tightrope walker

W

el windsurfing	el **ween**soorfeeng	windsurfing

Y

yo	**yo**	I, me
el yogur	el yo**goor**	yoghurt

Z

la zanahoria	la thana-**or**ee-a	carrot
las zapatillas	lass thapa**teel**yass	slippers
las zapatillas de deporte	lass thapa**teel**yass day de**por**tay	trainers
los zapatos	loss thapa**to**ss	shoes
los zorritos	loss tho**ree**toss	fox cubs
el zorro	el **thor**ro	fox
el zumo	el **thoo**mo	juice